INVOCATIONS OF LIGHT

INVOCATIONS OF LIGHT

Valdas Aušra

*Translated from the Lithuanian
by Jonas Zdanys*

Grey Willow Press

Translations Copyright © 2020 by Jonas Zdanys
Front cover photograph, *Højerup Gamle Kirke, Højerup, Denmark*,
copyright © Valdas Aušra
All Rights Reserved.

ISBN 978-1-7338882-5-7

Publication of this book was made possible by the generous encouragement and support of Konstantin Akhvlediani, Agne Paner, Lucy Siksnus, and the Lithuanian Lutheran Student Fund.

Manufactured in the United States of America

Grey Willow Press
greywillowpress.org
greywillowpress@gmail.com
Design by forgetgutenberg.com

Contents

The Guest / 1
They Say / 2
I Am / 3
We Go Toward Christmas / 4
What Is Christmas / 5
At Year's End / 6
Can... / 8
Prayer / 9
"I want to encourage you" / 10
Current / 11
"Many words remain unspoken" / 12
An Open Door / 14
"Every day awake in the morning" / 15
The River of Compassion / 17
The Cloud's Tear / 18
Prayer / 19
I Stopped In The Middle Of The Field / 20
My Heart / 21
Down On My Knees / 22
"Drops fall as it rains" / 23
"Why have the stars and moon darkened" / 24
Do Not Say / 25
I Am A Child of God / 26
Since I Was Young / 27
Drooping Arms / 28
I Will Pray... / 29
My Journey / 30
The Letter / 32
A Day's Journey / 33
Existence / 34
Forgive Me / 35
A Question / 36
Tell Me... / 37
Forgive Me, Lord / 38
Your Word / 39
Forgiveness / 40
Invitation / 42
Angel / 43
Stay With Me A While / 44

A Life Of Faith / 45
I Am Waiting / 46
How Great You Are / 47
I Am Human / 48
Word / 50
Overcast / 51
The Heart's Evening / 52
All Saints / 53
How? / 54
The Sounds Of Hymns / 55
Thank You / 56
What More Do I Need? / 57
"We do not know how to live waiting" / 58

The Guest

Tonight an unexpected guest came to see me
I knew at once that she was in the house
Unseen, unheard, only sensed
The air permeated with her presence
Frightened me
What do you want from me? I asked
I just wanted to see how you were doing
Why are you visiting me? It is not yet time
She did not answer.
What do I know?
Perhaps it is time to count the chickens?
Prepare the accounts?
Check how I am living?

Tonight I tossed back and forth in bed
Waking unexpectedly, groaning
Trying to understand
If there is something I still have to do here?
Or perhaps not?
If I think of some obligation or purpose
Would she leave me in peace? In escape?
But escape—why am I running?
From what? To what?
Only from myself, from You?
If only I would return to You, God…

When dawn of a new morning turned to light
The visitor left my room,
Only her faint scent
Dissolved in the air.
I lowered my feet to the ground
So I could again begin this new day given by God
Thanking Him and walking with firm steps
To share His many gifts.

They Say

They say that it snows sometimes
In the middle of a hot summer
And, reaching the ground, falls
On me, as if on a rock

They say that roses bloom sometimes
On Christmas in the cold
And melt the floes of ice
Thickened in the heart

They say that miracles happen
To us every day on our way
A child is born in a manger
So humankind would light its way

I Am

When I first wake I say good morning to the world
When I first wake I turn my eye to heaven
Traveling all day I repeat to myself
Today I am, I truly am myself

Meeting a glance, I open my own
Meeting a heart—I open the door
When I hear the voice I say to Him and to myself
Today I am, I truly am with You

And when the day ends, when the sun sets
My glance comes back pensively again
Down on my knees I repeat to You
Today I was, I am grateful that I am…

We Go Toward Christmas

We go toward Christmas through gray routine
Together with nature it embraces us
With a gray soiled weathered kerchief
Smelling of sorrow and camphor
It does not much warm our chilled bodies
We cover ourselves with it because nothing else remains
At the end of the day
Happiness only in remembrances
The sun only in memories

Warmth is only an echo in a distant forest
...only the concerns of Christmas preparations
Our steps are given inspiration
By fulfillment of our obligations
Waiting
Advent
As if a tied ferry is pulled by an invisible rope
Across a slow but powerfully flowing river
To the other shore
To the shore bright with the quiet joys of Christmas
Candles
Warmth
Light, which darkness cannot cover
Which the gray kerchief cannot grant
The joy of being together
Conferring strength and courage, and hope
Leading us through darkness and bringing us to light
The light of congregation
The light of birth
The light of rebirth
Life
A new life and beginning
With loved ones
With nature
With heaven...

What Is Christmas

Days contract completely in winter
It is the cold that affects them so
The lifelike expression of inorganic chemistry
Lessens among the elements of molecules
Compensating in the cold and energy lost at night
Of course, we are talking about the days
And they are made of hours, minutes and seconds
Which pull back from the cold and nesting into themselves shorten
Light decreases and shortens
The day shortens
And shortening pulls the night onto itself
And compensating for its diminution lengthens the night...

What should a person do in such a time?
We sleep more and much longer
Though the nights are much longer than our sleep
That is why we learned to use fire
It shines in the dark shortening the night
That is why we learned to light the lamp
So it would shine when there is no sun or fire
So it would lengthen the light between molecules and seconds
Through the longest night we celebrate Christmas
So with the help of created light we could help organic light to live
So it would conquer darkness
So day would not contract into one small point
So the black hole would not be created
...
So life would continue

Christmas—the birth day of the light of life...

At Year's End

At the end of the year thoughts begin on their own to lay out periods
Accents, exclamation marks, commas, question marks or ellipses
They leaf through the journal of daily reflections
Beginning with the clearest pages
Nuzzle through them trying to find what has already faded
And to renew the colors
Revive them
Refresh neuronal synaptic connections
To the surface rise pictures in sentiment's lifegiving colors
Sounds that had already sunk to the bottoms of drawers
Fragrances once again filling the room
Brimming with emotions, experiences lifted from archives
Those histories that hid on the surface
Leading down narrow labyrinthine pathways toward others
More deeply hidden in memory's layers
Some had slid there on their own
Because they were not important
Only that day's or moment's ordinary photograph
Now already not saying anything
All that remains is to ask why it has not yet been torn up
And just takes up space…
Perhaps now I do not understand its significance…
Other moments find themselves there deliberately
Hidden
Closed away
Even locked up
So they do not rise to the surface
So they do not disturb the scenes of a beautiful life's painting
So they do not injure with their sharp edges
The hands and fingers of those who leaf through them
The eyes, the ears, and even the souls
Or even more simply — if people see it
What would they think or say?
That is why we hide everything that gives us pain
Under heavy locks
In the darkest corners of dark cellars…

At the end of the year standing near the manger
You understand that there is nothing you can hide
And all that you try to hide rises to the surface
And reveals itself in me, like a reflection in a mirror
Only a single hope remains and it is the birth of the child
The birth of the one who died on the cross for you
And by his birth, as in his death,
Gave you a new white beginning
To begin the year anew
Not afraid of the labyrinths of memory
Hidden pain or darkness
The child was born for you! ...

Can...

Can ice warm us?
I ask myself
even if the cold inside
is greater than the brook turned to glass

Can heat cool?
I cannot doubt that
because even the heart frozen in ice trembles
remembering the heat of love's wave
that slackened when hands united

What remains true
and what does not change
is memory, faith and love
the third — love — is eternal

Prayer

I thank You, God, each day
For the sun, the sky, the earth
For the family that surrounds us
For the scarf of the comforts of home

That covers not just our shoulders
But also gently wrapped
Gives warmth to the heart
Calms impulsive thoughts

I thank You, because You embrace us
In Your arms of grace
In the light of the Son's birth
The danger of the cross grows pale…

I want to encourage you
So you would remain in that place
To which you were brought by God
And would live everything out to the end
Accepting that what has been given
Is perhaps joy or perhaps suffering
Because you do not know what may open
In the field of your eyes or beating heart

I ask and encourage you
To accept the lessons meant for you
Not rejecting a single experience
Not even those you think are not needed
Though it could be the one that holds
Two or three shores in single union

Come, stop, and remain in the point
In time and space assigned to you on life's journey
In the union of feeling and thought
With your existence in God
And in the world He has created,
Which is meant for you
So that having experienced all of being
You could be the salt of life for others.

Current

Stop for a moment on the banks of the river
With its current begin your journey
Swilling the damp congealed banks
Your spouting energy will curl across the rocks
Rolling out thin blades of sand

Smooth the stone on the bottom
With the soft current that embraces everything
So it would fit fully into the child's hand
And night would tell him stories

About the sources of the stream, which hurry
Over trees stumps, earth lumps and crags
Always running and not able to stop
With its soft power razing obstructions
Carrying a drop so it would melt in the sea

About the colors of water, rock and cloud
Grass and trees growing on the banks
Wading to the knees or diving under
Color the currents that flow in the sky

About fish immersed in the current
With polished scales reflecting the stars
Rising from pools to listen to the moon
Sing hymns that cannot be heard with the ears

And about how the waters unite
All of us with one another
Across grass, fish, rock and humankind itself
The flowing current of life...

Many words remain unspoken
Some I did not say
    because I was afraid
    of hurting someone dear to me
Others my lips could not utter
    because a small word
        could return in an avalanche of snow
        sweeping everything in its way

still other words,
    like stones,
        remained deep inside of me and besieged my heart—
        do not allow it to beat, flutter
I stay quiet, my lips tightly pressed
    so they would not escape
clenching my teeth
    even if they crumble
        just so no moan or lament,
        anger and pain, and hatred would erupt
            like a bullet exploding everything it strikes

Because much has been said
    that has hurt
        that burned like phosphorus
            spattered like dirt
                tore, broke, devastated, tortured
tell me—what should I do with the words
    mouldering in my heart and mind?

In the tingling silence of being
    the murmur of peace rang out
In that silence I saw God's mute Word
It hung on the cross
    drops of blood dripped
        and splashed on clods of dirt
            poured out in my eyes
                tongue, body, heart and mind

the stones melted
        constricting the heart, conscience, freedom
my lips burned
        uttering the Word:
                repentance, forgiveness, LOVE.

An Open Door

An open door
the freshness of wind
fills the house
airs out the corners
chases stirs incites
the stupor of the air
to move and us

Open hands
have something to give
because they accepted
what was given
what was shared
with them
to increase, like the fish
distributed, like the bread
to embrace when the perished
son returns

Open ears
opened eyes
when they hear
they immediately see
Your Word
bearing life
in the valley of bones
life awakens
the heart's hardness
ruptures from love

If hearts are open, he will knock
Even God cannot enter hearts that are closed

Every day awake in the morning
I begin my journey
which leads me through emotions
experiences feelings
through cold and heat
love and hatred
through words and sounds
and silence
through people near and far
known and not at all familiar

Everything
that I experience on my journey
settles on my clothing,
hands and face, hair,
penetrates my eyes and ears,
mouth and nostrils,
and through them
—ever deeper—
like an enemy's reconnaissance
intrudes inward
and lies down in memory's dressers,
covers itself in emotions' sheets,
nuzzles to the depths of the heart.

The journey through the day
becomes a field of battle.
I—a warrior,
prepared to defend against attack.
Where are my weapons?
What will help me fight?
Where are my enemies?
Where do I find allies?
What will protect me
so I do not perish?
God, HELP ME!

The word rings out in the journey's darkness—
You are my child!
Take and eat!
Take and drink!
My sluggish heart begins to relax,
the rock of ice begins to melt
and life diffuses through my
body like water springs,
hurricanes of thought quiet,
memory's opened doors
remind me—
He has not abandoned me,
He stood guard,
when I hid locked in fear
in the fortress.

At the end of day
when my journey is over
my heart open to You without fear,
I will fall asleep in the embrace of bliss...

The River of Compassion

The river of compassion flows through me
The current courses unstopping, powerful
Gushing in springs from the Lord's wounds
Dripping from the curse of the dried tree
And splashing reddish purple on the rock
Lifting to life the heart pressed in death's hand
One…another…an infinite number…

Tiny drop after tiny drop
The spring brooks in a stream to a river
Through every faithful heart
As if through a meadow to a road
That leads us all to a heavenly home
Though the Word, baptism and communion in bread and wine
Community one with another and with the Most High
Through His grace…

The river of compassion having spurted out in Eden's Garden,
Having absorbed a drop of the blood of the cross,
Flows through you, through me and Him,
Washing clean the wounds and dust of life
And preparing the wedding feast of the Lamb…

The Cloud's Tear

When clouds float past the windows
Light is reflected from them
Pouring out a drop of the green sea
The color of moss into my eye

From the depths of that drop emerge the pains
Of childhood, trampled hopes, lost rejoicings
Something that hides in the forgotten
Corners of the time that has passed

Do not be afraid to look through the window into my eyes
Do not be afraid to open the window to the rain
Because everything that is hidden or forgotten
Finds its existence in the light of day
And does not frighten us any longer...

Prayer

A word rose from the depths
held my throat
thrashes between my lips
it seems it may soon fall
and crumble
only shards will be left to gather

A feeling arose in my heart
and lifted in my chest
like a tongue of flame
gathered in my eyes
it seems it will soon scatter
in droplet streams

For a brief moment
time stopped
everything congealed, all that lived
but from the very bottom
as if through a tunnel
breaking through the ice
and stone walls
emerged
a prayer

And the word
became flesh
and a tear
moistened my cheeks
my knees bent
and my lowered head
reached the dust of the road

AH, DO NOT FORSAKE ME

I Stopped In The Middle Of The Field

I stopped in the middle of the field
I cannot take another step
My legs will not lift
My arms hang down
My whole body has congealed
I search for my own roots—but do not find them

Where are you my roots?
Nourish me!
I am thirsty!
I stand as dried
As wormwood in the wind
Embittered
Disillusioned
Cast by the wind
Looking for peace in myself...alas...

Come to me
You bringer of peace
Revive me with the word
Your love
And a ray of familiar being
Light my darkness
Abate my thirst with wine
And bread—my hunger
So I could once again here sing
Hymns
Of hope faith and love

My Heart

My heart will be a home for you
My thought a path leading you home
My life, dedicated to you alone
And my words—a hymn of gratitude

I will return home on the paths of reflection
I will unite two shores with a bridge of faith
I will vanquish all of the deserts of existence
Looking at the serpent on the staff

Today I will begin the day anew
With repetence and gratitude on my lips
With a heart filled, overflowing with joy
Not afraid to break one more time in suffering.

Down on My Knees

Down on my knees
I pray to you Lord
I turn to you
Because I was blinded
I do not see that road
That stretches ahead
Do not see the direction
Toward which I walked

Down on my knees
My head bowed low
I cannot lift
My eyes to you
Because I still carry in my heart
Hidden from you
The darkest hatred
Which I can raise
To no one to no one

Down on my knees
I understand—I am sinful
And not worthy of the grace
You give to others
But collapsed beneath the cross
I still pray—help me
Do not turn away from me
The watchful look of your eyes...

Drops fall as it rains
Tap tap tap
On the dried out ground
The earth's cracked skin
      slowly closes up
Wounds heal and scars vanish—
      slowly slowly they narrow
Tap tap tap
Until not a trace remains

Drops fall as it rains
Until they heal the earth's wounds
Tap tap tap
And reach the seed hidden deep below.
The dried sliver swells
Life hiding in the depths awakens
And breaking through the coffin's boards
Shoots up to freedom
Tap tap tap
The delicate sprout raises its head.

Tap tap tap
Drops of life fall
Rivers flow down windows
Tears—down cheeks
Tap tap tap
Wounds mend
The body heals
Death withdraws
Tap tap tap
That which had died
Resurrects to life.

Why have the stars and moon darkened
        Why is the gloomy sky so threatening
                rain already washing my face?
Perhaps it is my own tears
        having broken out of the soul's labyrinths
                that have erupted in a loud lament?

A bird took wing
        frightened by my lament
                screaked thrashing on a tree branch
                        disappearing in the dead of night
spring buds lowered their heads
        trembling in fright
                wept straight through
who can measure the depths of sorrow?
who can stop the lament
why have you forsaken me, God?

...

    the storm menacing crawled beyond the forest
    rain washing my face calmed down
    the bowed blossom timidly lifted
    the morning dawn marked
            that the sun is still alive
    and the grave empty
    the frightened bird returns to its nest.

Do Not Say...

Do not say,
Do not say you're going
But come down the road
Come over the meadow or sea
Wade across the stream...

Do not say,
Do not say you are longing
That is it is painful...frightening
But open your heart to me
I will touch you with my wing...

Do not say,
Do not say you love me,
Just come...open
Look into my eyes—
I will accept you as you are...

Afraid...
In pain...
With drooping arms...
Wounded and bloody...
Like the crucified
Who died for me...

I Am A Child Of God

I am a child of God
Who can say otherwise?
Who can deny that I belong to Him?
Even when I pull away from Him
Even then when, angry, I turn my back
Or when, paying no attention,
I think only about myself forgetting Him
Or my brother...

I am a child of God
Imperfect, full of shortcomings
Not worthy to be a citizen of the kingdom
Sometimes pouring anger on my neighbor
Or even specially wishing or creating evil...
Knowing feeling and longing for closeness
Protection, that I am not worthy of...

I am a child of God
Because He loves me
As I am, with my failings
Covered in the dirt of sin
Blind, angry, tired of loving
My neighbor or even Him Himself

I am a child of God
Undeserving of His love
A healed leper perhaps turning back
To worship and thank...
A prodigal son, awaited for his return
To the open embrace of grace
Spattered with the blood of the cross...

Since I Was Young

Since I was young
Since I was born
I have loved life
And have grabbed it
With all my strength
And cunning and wisdom
Hungered to know it with all my essence.
I was angry with it
When it scolded me,
But in secret
And sometimes loudly, said to it,
I long for caresses!

My arms spread wide
I wanted to embrace, press close
Absorb like nectar into myself
And enjoy every one of its fragrances
Sounds, small pains in the skin
Or smarting of the heart…
I want to drown in it, sink down
Breathe every second given to me
And not lose a single minute,
Not miss an hour…

The joys of life are equally
Important to me as its pains
Clear skies as much as storms
Given my life—
And you cannot refuse such gifts!
I will accept everything
That you give me
Even death
Because I believe that it
Is truly not the end…

Drooping Arms

Lift your drooping arms,
Because I want to give you a gift.
Lift them at least to your chest!
I will fill them
With the joys of life
And the pains of love and strength

I will give you everything
You will need
To travel life's road bravely.
Just make room in your arms
So I would have room
To put it all...

Do not be afraid to open your shirt
So my gifts
Will touch your naked body—
Only an open heart can accept
Without precondition
Everything everything, even nettles...

Just lift your drooping arms
So I could give you hope.
Stretch out your hands—
I will fill them with the sap of life
Which will raise you and let you walk.

Just lift your drooping arms...

I Will Pray ...

I will pray for you my sister
so you would love your life
so while you hand out handfuls of sun
you will not forget to lift up yourself

I will pray for you my brother
so you would accept the love meant for you
so while you sacrifice your own day
you will not forget to take your measure

I will pray for you my child
so you would grow up having a heart
that will have sympathy for those you meet
so when you grow up you will not judge others

I will pray for you o world
so you would not murder your children
so you would not condemn, would not battle
but will care for and embrace

Pray for me my sister
Pray for me my brother
so I would protect my beating heart
so I will not turn into stone...

My Journey

I became an old
        rough bed sheet
kept in
a dresser drawer
just because I reminded
someone of nights
slept covered with me
in a made bed
just because
someone was caressed on me
loved
because
I drank the sweat of summer
and love
because I smelled clean
when laid upon

today they found it
        in the corner of the drawer
and tore it into strips
        —a wound opened for someone
and cherry drops scattered;
someone's heart tore in half
        unable to bear it
—let us use the sheet
to stop the drops
maintain the heart in unity

I am a small roadside stone
kicked by travelers
        back and forth
shortening and clarifying
the gloomy and difficult journey.

I am God's
        vessel
filled with compassion
Through His grace
        I am what I am.

I know only
that on this journey
      I can serve Him
as an old sheet
      and small stone
because when it ends
      I will once again find peace
In His loving embrace.

The Letter

Death is my friend
She wrote me a letter
How she misses
Our visits together
How when we meet we talk or sing
How we see each other without falsehood

Shoulders pressed together in one room
We remember the time that has passed
Plucking a grass stem by the wide road
We will string together one and another memory
A necklace hung on the gates of life

Death is my friend
She wrote me a letter
The beads from the grass stem
Scattered on the dirt floor...

A Day's Journey

When evening draws near, I'll turn my steps toward home
when evening draws near and my eyes get drowsy and can't see
in which direction to go, where to turn, and fear tickles my heart,
I'll pause to consider the day and my experiences on this journey

where I had traveled, what I saw and learned, and what I gathered
I will pull all my discoveries from my rucksack and gifts given on
        the way
is what I find in the bag of my days worth the effort to carry it?
I do not know that today because I have not seriously checked
        that bag, just understand somewhat

I just know that the road started in the morning is not long—
        know that truly
and my steps have already been counted, I just do not know that
        yet
as the rucksack gets heavier my steps shorten and slow—my pace
        has changed
perhaps it is worth giving away what is in the bag to others, so I
        will not slow?

and the time to return relentlessly comes and invites reflections on
        what I learned
the journey will lengthen, leaving behind the common and the
        fences of matter
the shorter the steps in the commonplace, the more powerful the
        thought
until it is time to return to the home where my path first began…

Existence

The heat of your day
Burned away all that wasn't real
Left only the essence of existence

The foundation on which life stands
Is not built with my hands
It is much stronger than a ray of the sun

Come and see, the drop of blood spattered
In love falling on the dried ground
Opening new life for the world

Forgive Me

I moan in a muffled voice
because the howler's stone heated
burned my heart to the very blood
it sipped heat into itself like salt
not created by the sun, but...

It is better to pour out
my stresses like this
than to burn my loved ones
with the volcanic lava of my emotions

Forgive me, I did not know otherwise
I will fall brother sister beneath your feet
and pray for your forgiveness,
so the wounds I gave you
would heal without leaving scars...

A Question

I want to pose a question,
Just cannot manage to formulate it...
What is it about?
Perhaps the people surrounding me?
Where are they from?
Why did I meet them on the road of my life?
Why do some of them come with me for just a short while
      While others for my whole life—even after death?

I want to ask about human choice,
Why are we able to choose?
Do we truly have that freedom?
But perhaps it is just an illusion,
      In which it is so easy to get lost...
I have come to more than one crossroad
chose a direction
the decision in some was easy for me and heady,
at others I suffered, doubted and lingered

I will pose a question about life, its purpose
Is it true that every life has a purpose?
A snake's, bird's, worm's, or cat's?
And a human's?
It destoys those who disturb it
      or do not provide benefit
why are we allowed to be creators
      though we create from that which already is

I want to ask, why did You create me?

Tell Me...

Tell me
Why did you leave turning away your face?
Why does the shirt shine white in the distance
Having absorbed my sweat?
You led me to the wilderness and left me
When I wanted to soak in the water
And catch fish with a full haul

Tell me
Why did you show me the azure sky
Why did you tempt my meditating eyes
To lift from the earth to the wide horizon
You promised to give me wings
Even though I have sunken my roots deep in the soil?

Tell me
Why I believed
Why, leaving the meadows and green forests,
I followed into my own wilderness wanting to know you
Looking for those promised wings

Forgive Me, Lord

Forgive me, Lord, that I have not shown my face in so long
In Your house, which stands silent and empty,
That I have forgotten how hymns to You are sung
And how to turn to You in prayer...

I had run off to search for myself
In the wide world with wide roads,
I wanted to find a place for myself under the sun,
Believed—without me no one would find it...

I believed it was meant for me
To pull the world out of its hole—
Just walk that step and stretch out my hand,
In that way distract humankind safely
From the steps taken to the abyss...

Forgive me, Lord, ...I could not do it...
And lost return to You,
So I would feel safe in Your sanctuary
And would learn to sing once more to Your glory,
Would repeat words of repentence, my heart's prayers...

To thank You for shedding Your blood
And with love pulling me from that abyss,
Accompanying me on mistaken roads and waiting
Patiently for me to come home to the source of being...

Your Word

Raised by Your word
I want to open my heart to You
Say everything everything
Not just what presses on it
But all that I sank and hide
In its bottomless depths

Touched by Your hands
I want to open my own
So I could press against my breast
Those who sorrow in loneliness
Longing for intimacy

I will revive my heart
With Your words will prepare it
So I will be able to accept
Being close to a beloved one

I will press them to my heart
I will nourish them with Your words
I will revive them with Your words
I will disseminate Your love

Forgiveness

> *Then Peter came to Him and said, "Lord, how often shall my brother sin against me, and I forgive him? Up to seven times?" Jesus said to him, "I do not say to you, up to seven times, but up to seventy times seven."*
> Matthew 18:21-22

How many times do I have to forgive my brother?
Once a disciple asked of the Lord.
He wanted to know if there was a limit
At which he could slam shut the door
And not let his brother into the home of his heart.

This world teaches
That everything has a beginning
A stormy period of life, or perhaps calm,
And a painful ending...
And beyond it there is nothing...

And in the end—let's consider this carefully—
It is too hard to forgive the one
Who has trespassed against you, hurt or betrayed you...
And what if he does not beg me for forgiveness?
Even though I am good, I cannot always forgive!

Would it be enough to do so seven times?
Seven—the number of perfection
Having come to us from the dead of ages.
Seven, the number of completion.
It is enough, God, right? And it is easy to count...

I am not saying to you—up to seven,
But up to seventy times seven,
An answer so unexpected rang in my ears
And, flowing down signal neurons,
Fell straight into my heart like a hot coal

And God wants perfection not created by man!
He asks us to behave as He does
Forgive the sins of others, as mine are also

Forgiven, each day anew!
Because I am washed by the blood of the lamb
White white and left without objection...

So I hurry to disseminate forgiveness
To the traveler met on the road,
I call him brother, invite him in;
I give the sweet water of life to the thirsty,
Cut a slice of bread for the hungry
And put it from my hand into his
I bend by the bed of the sick
And comfort in the loss of pain...
Though I have nothing with which to comfort
And only give what I have generously received
From the Lord's open bloody hands

Invitation

Come, o Lord, to my paradise
And stay living here forever
I long so much to see You in my gardens
And continue our talk begun long ago

I would teach You how to make cheese
From apples picked from that other appletree
And ask You once again to prune the tree
Whose branches no longer carry fruit

Come, o Lord, to our paradise
Taste my mother's home pressed cheese with us
Flavored with the bitter salt of life
We place it on the altar in front of You

Come, o Lord, and stay with us
Singing together we will plant our orchards
Together we will prune their branches and pick their fruits
And eating the cheese will remember paradise
That always awaits children who return...

Angel

Did you see your angel today?
Did you remember to turn to him?
He stands cowering outside the door
And does not dare come in

He is ready to extend his wing
When you fall on the angled road
Will go with you through the dark ravine
When you lay on your death bed

Will you remember that your angel
Is meant to protect your day
He sees every one of your steps
Just you open that door to him

Stay With Me A While

Stay with me a while,
stay just a bit longer, even a minute
if you can't go with me to eternity
even a second spent with you, when eternity is open
to time, space and thought
or perhaps it is not a thought
perhaps it is only a moment taking the form of a cloud on the road
and a ray of sun
warming the dew-covered garden in the morning
and the wet fallen apples...

Stay with me a while
in the eternal continuation of a moment
congealed time embraced
           eyes, ears and our existence
It is really not important
what hides beyond the boundary
dividing us between here and there
what will remain — is an apple
covered in orchard leaves and
having captured a ray of sun inside itself

Stay with me a while
do not move your lips away
from my forehead hot
      with the passionate running of the day
those lips that stop the flow of time
      and save me
protect me from the madness
      of this day

Stay with me a while
and may time stop
together with existence in the blink
of every second

A Life of Faith

Faith is like life
It pulsates through the whole body
And forces you to move forward
Especially when I pray
Down on my knees
My forehead touching the dust

I Am Waiting...

I sit in the dark with eyes closed
Try to hear what the silence is saying
My entire body tense I listen
If I might hear the coming light
Ready to release the inner spring
And begin my life. The new one...

How Great You Are...

How great You are, God
Accepting everyone
      even those who, excluding others
Want to keep You for themselves
Our fences do not keep You out
      boundary markers, road signs
          rules

You open your hands
      pierced with our nails
and with the cross embrace
      all of us all of us
Even those who do not know You
      who want to deny that You exist

How great you are, Lord,
You give the sun, rain, harvest
      to all to all
          who live on the earth
Good evil
      who believe or who deny
          who are blind or who search for a future

Your generosity amazes me
It is difficult for me to believe
How different our viewpoints are
Who is dear to us, who is not
Who carried the flag of love
      and who only suffering
Who comes to bow before You
      near the sources of existence

How great you are, God
Accepting me, who has sinned
Hands are pressed together in repentance
Fly here like a spirit
The way way wind flies
Make my life
      a song of the heart

I Am Human

I am human
That means that I am not perfect
Not sensitive enough to others
Egotistically looking out for my needs
Even the saints in pictures, even they
Press their hands together on their breasts
In prayer toward themselves...

But I, o God, am not a saint
I have sinned...
In thought word deed
What I have done
Or did not do when I needed to do it
Or what I have said...
Or did not say when I needed to speak
What I have thought or craved or been angry...

But God, You know
I seek perfection
I do not believe I know
Where this desire comes from
I only want to stand by
Your altar
And sing eternal glory to You

I am only guessing, God,
That it is perhaps because I am created
In the image of Your son?
And the memory
Of days in the garden of paradise
Hides in the marrow of my bones?

And God, You know
My sin and my desire
You knew me
Even before I was born
And called me to life
You sacrified Your son
So Your paling spirit

Would awaken in me
And would invite me to return home
To You...

I am a man created by Your love...

Word

The word from your mouth
Hung congealed in the coldness of space
And pierced the heart like a crystal of ice

The letter of the law can only kill
It draws boundaries as if walls
Without feeling, without tremblings of the heart

It falls like a millstone on the feet
Pressing the toes
Does not allow a single step to the side

Hands and feet flooded with blood
The day's sweat drips to the earth
Pressing steps and eyes to the ground

Lift your eyes to the sunfilled sky
Turn your eye of perception inside
There where the injured heart bleeds

And accept the healing word
Which proclaims to you and to others
News in the market square

Blood was shed on the cross
The grave is already empty—only linens remain
It is not necessary to sacrifice yourself on the altars of gods

Overcast...

Overcast days
Overcast thoughts
Overcast heart
Turned my eyes to under my feet
Looking for cracks in the asphalt path
That would lead me to Your depths
Rendering clear water
That calms my life in the wilderness

The Heart's Evening

Evening crept in slowly
In lengthening shadows under the bushes
And the muffling songs of crickets
In the yard spreading a path of colored leaves

Night's coolness wound its arms around my shoulders
Her cold fingers pressed against my body
And caused me to shrink into myself
Looking for warmth in the depths of my heart

It is that place where two worlds meet
There leaves fallen to the ground
Dream of the explosions of buds
Not yet born in a drop of autumn rain

But everything that has withered or frozen dies
And cannot find the road back again
Finds a new beginning in the center of the heart
When God's endless love touches it

All Saints

Through meadows wet with tears
I wade toward a copse of lifted trees
Lost in the expanse of bare fields
In the shadows of its trees generations
Of forefathers laying embraced by covetous sand
Invite us to visit the chopped down gardens
Already decaying on the edges of memory
Cottages of moiled clay already undone
Lilacs gone wild calling out
In the trills of lost nightingales
Jurgutis has long since stopped bridling the horses
The scythe has rusted at the edge of the field
Its bones laid in our forefathers' fertilized soil
Patiently waiting for guests...

How?

How can I thank you for this day?
Because when I wake I rejoice in a ray of sunlight
When, whisking through the colors of autumn leaves,
It leaps from the windowsill and stops on my palm
Warms my fingers, arms, body
And plants a sprout of joy in my thoughts.
The coffee beans are already ground
Their aroma, spreading through the house,
      fills every corner and crack
As if by accident met a sun bunny in the doorway
And the house blossomed with the colors of fall...
How do I thank you for this amazing day?...

The Sounds of Hymns

The sounds of hymns
Invaded my thoughts
Cleansed the gloomy corners of my heart
Opened my stony lips
And lifted my eyes toward heaven

The sounds of hymns
Painted my heavens
With the clearest colors
That I had never seen before
Scattered the storm's somber clouds
And invited my thoughts to fly on paths of stars

The sounds and words of hymns
Brought me to prayer
And moved my heart toward God
The sounds of hymns
Built a strong bridge
Uniting two separate shores

The sounds of hymns
Like a key unlatched
What once had been locked up…

Thank You

I think the time has come to express my thanks
I have not decided yet for what
Most likely it should be...for myself?
And why not?
Because I live, because I have a roof over my head,
Because my own roof "has not yet receded,"
Because the smell of turkey tickles my nose.
For the glass of wine and the heat it raises.
Because the fireplace flame attracts my glance
And stops my thought.

I am thankful for the family in which I grew up;
For the family in which I live.
For the people who raised me
From my birth until right now.
For those who gave me the day's most bitter lessons
And those who loved me, love and will love,
Who went with me on my journey when I did not want to go,
Or it was too difficult to take that step
Who did not sleep at night—
Who prayed for me when I strayed.

I could thank God
That I am,
Who made it possible for me to appear
And experience everything
That I can be thankful for, that I have.
That for me and for my loved ones
He created Earth, Sun, and Universe
And ripened the grain of rye in the soil
So there would be enough bread
On mankind's table or the Altar.
I am thankful for the sacrifice of the cross
Whose shed blood
Cleanses everything on which it falls,
Grants hope
Gives me eyes of faith
And teaches me to love myself, you and Him.

What More Do I Need?

A loaf of barley bread
Fish on the table—
What more do I need
To be happy?

Perhaps only hands
Roughened by work
Which, when just touching,
Would lift toward God...

We do not know how to live waiting
We do not need to wait for the yearlings to grow
Until the crops swim across the fields
And corn ripens in its ears
Satisfying our hunger each day
Supplementing the strengths of our bodies
That we use to encounter the coming day
To fulfill our jobs, raise our children
Or extending a hand or opening our hearts
To nourish a hungry fellow traveler on our journey

We do not know how to patiently wait
For that which nature, man or God had begun
We do not have the patience to wait for the miracle
Until the plant grown from the grain ripens
Or leavening, moved by warmth, prepares the dough
To turn into bread, steaming on the table
Tempting us with its fragrance to come and sit around it
To reflect on the day moving toward its ending
Together share it like a sacrament
Breaking off a bit and placing it in the hand
Of the family member sitting alongside
Mother, brother, child, spouse
Or perhaps a neighbor who has dropped by
Because she needed a pinch of salt
While making supper in her own home

Let us call together all those met during the day
To pass a little while together, to not hurry
And let us give without begrudging ourselves
Patiently, bit by bit, not worrying if we get back
Let us not hurry ...And we will see
How the grain that died in autumn
Raises the rye and becomes ten more new grains
How the milled rye over time becomes bread
Feeding throngs of people
How by giving your day bit by bit to others
You miraculously gain the wisdom of their days
And that short day of life
Suddenly turns into ten days...

www.ingramcontent.com/pod-product-compliance
Lightning Source LLC
Chambersburg PA
CBHW021132080526
44587CB00012B/1248